Diet recommendations for TCM - Lung - Yin deficiency

Please check these recommendations always with a nutrition consultant, therapist, doctor or dietician. The recipes and the list of ingredients are supporting the conventional medical therapy.
The calorie disclosures of fresh ingredients (fruit and vegetables) vary according to quality and time of harvest. The contents were checked by a dietician and a nutrition consultant for the Traditional Chinese Medicine (TCM).

Author:
©2019 Josef Miligui
www.ebns.at

AF206442

Source:
The lists are created from the EBNS database for nutritional counseling. The database is used by dietitians, therapists and doctors for advising the patient / client.

Literature:
The specialist literature and the training documents of the German and Austrian dietary and traditional Chinese medicine serve as a knowledge base. We have used the documents as a basis of knowledge, adapted it to our experience and completed them.
http://di-book.com

Production and publishing:
BoD – Books on Demand, Norderstedt
ISBN: 9783746097411

Diet recommendations for TCM - Lung - Yin deficiency

1 Treatment strategy

Nourish and moisturize lung yin, strengthen middle, nourish kidney yin.
Hot NO, warm LITTLE, neutral and refreshing YES, cold LITTLE

2   Avoid

Bitter or dehydrating food, beverages, alcohol, sake, lamb, turkey, hot and hot spices, very salty (sausage, cheese, ham, smoked), grilled, deep-fried, dry air, climate, screen , Smoking, synthetic fibers.

3   Breakfast

kkal. per serving

Adzuki Bean and Rice Soup	199
Apple sauce with raisins	73
Breakfast - Rice with fruits	230
Buddhist reissue soup	279
Celery juice	33
Coconut water	30
Cooling rice dish with grapefruit	234
Cous-Cous with date, coco and almondpuree	483
Cucumber soup	95
Curdcheesedumplings on strawberry pulp	553
Grape juice with hot water	43
Hungarian rice salad	421
Italian champignon rice	256
Millet with egg and butter	338
Miso soup with tofu	51
Oyster mushrooms with asparagus	316
Pear compote	100
Pear juice	180
Radish with sugar	46
Radishjuice	9
Reissue soup with duck	160
Rice congee with honey pear and black sesame	158
Roasted millet with Celery sticks	400
Roasted nuts	973
Spelled-grid porridge with berries of the season	243
Tea from celery sticks	0
Tea from coriander	2
Tea from marshmallow tea	0
Tea from peppermint with white sugar	7
Tea from red dates	12
Tsampa with jam or fruit compote	280
Vegetable miso soup with tofu	106
Wheat fresh grain porridge with pears	309

4 Snack

5 Lunch

6 Afternoon

7 Dinner

8   Any time

9 Recipes

(rec.) = You can use more.
(little) = You should use less than specified
(omit) = omit.

9.1 8 treasures of rice

Strengthens kidney and bladder, builds up Qi, strengthens the spleen, repels moisture, reduces internal heat, builds heart, calms nerves.
Cooking time approx. 1 hour
Calories p. portion: 223
4 portions

Quantity of ingredients:
Lily bulbs 1 table spoon / 5g. () - cool - sweet, bitter .... *
Longane 1 table spoon / 5g. (little) - warm - sweet.. *
King Solomon's-seal 1 table spoon / 5g. () - neutral - sweet, bitter .... *
Yam root, yam root tuber 1 table spoon / 5g. () - neutral - sweet .... *
Coix (seeds) YiYi Ren 1 table spoon / 5g. (yes) - cool - sweet, neutral............ *
Rice wild (nature rice) 1 1/2 cups / 240g. (rec.) - neutral - sweet, bitter .... metal
Water 8-10 cups / 800g. (yes) - cool - salty..earth

Cooking instructions:
Each one 1 tbsp: Bai He, Longan, Yu Zhu, Da Zao, Shan Yao, Lian Mi, Yi Yi Ren, Qian Shi
Add hot water and soak for about 30 minutes. Then add 1 - 2 cups of rice (normal) and simmer for 1/2 to 1 hour until the rice is very soft. Or: Cook for about 3 hours with the herbs a congee. Then the herbs do not have to be soaked.

9.2 Adzuki Bean and Rice Soup

Reduces moisture, directs down, reduces gastrointestinal heat, builds up essence, strengthens muscles after heat illness, builds up body fluids.
Cooking time approx. 2 hours
Calories p. portion: 199
1 portion

Quantity of ingredients:
Adzuki beans 8 table spoons / 40g. (yes) - neutral - sweet, sour .... water
Rice round grain 2 table spoons / 20g. (rec.) - neutral - sweet.................. metal
Water 1 1/2 cups / 200g. (yes) - cool - salty ....earth
Honey 1 table spoon / 8g. (rec.) - cold - sweet...earth

Cooking instructions:
Boil soaked adzuki beans and round grain rice in a ratio of 4: 1 in water until a thin pulp has formed. Sweet as needed; possibly puree.

Effect: This recipe strengthens kidney, spleen and stomach and is particularly suitable for mothers with too little milk flow.

9.3 Apple sauce with raisins

Nourishes fluids, reduces stomach heat, strengthens spleen, harmonizes stomach, moisturizes, relaxes, builds up Qi.
Cooking time approx. 25 min
Calories p. portion: 74
10 portions
Allergens: O

Quantity of ingredients:
Apple (sweet) 2,2 lbs / 1000g. (rec.) - cool - sweet, sour ....earth
Water 1/2 cup / 100g. (yes) - cool - salty...earth
Raisins 1/8 lbs - 2oz / 50g. (little) - warm - sweet.......................................earth

Cooking instructions:
Wash, peel and quarter the apples and remove the core. Put the apples with the water in a pot. Wash the raisins with hot water and add them. Cook at low heat for about 10 minutes, then allow to cool. For children up to 10 months, mash in the blender finely. For the larger ones, crush with the potato steamer. Fill and seal in a freezer or empty yoghurt jug. Close the yoghurt jug. Freeze in the shock freezer.
If necessary, thaw at room temperature for about 6 hours. (Lasting about 4 months).
The fruit mousse is intended as dessert or intermediate meal. It has an anti-digestive effect. In case of diarrhea give better banana.

9.4 Basic recipe for a chicken broth worming

Strengthens Qi and blood, is very warm.
Cooking time approx. 2-3 hours
Calories p. portion: 90
9 portions
Allergens: L

Quantity of ingredients:

Chicken meat 1/2 piece / 600g. (little) - warm - sweet............................... wood
Carrot 2 pieces / 150g. (yes) - neutral - sweet ....earth
Leek 1 stick / 45g. (little) - warm - acrid.. metal
Celery root 1 piece / 500g. (rec.) - cool - sweet...earth
Ginger fresh 2 slices / 2g. (little) - warm - acrid... metal
Juniper berry 1 teaspoon / 3g. (omit) - warm - sweet, acrid, bitter ....fire
Bay leaf 3 pieces / 2g. () - warm - acrid... metal
Water 4 cup / 900g. (yes) - cool - salty...earth

Cooking instructions:

Remove chicken parts from fat. Place chicken pieces in a saucepan
with hot water and heat till it boils briefly, skimming any resulting foam.
Add coarsely chopped vegetables and all spices and cook over medium
heat for 2 to 3 hours. Strain the finished soup. Throw away vegetables
and bones.
Tip: If you want to use the meat as a soup insert, take out after 45
minutes and return only the bones in the soup.
Refrigerate for later use.

9.5   Basic recipe for a reissue soup (Congee)

Warms the stomach and spleen, harmonizes the intestine, forces Qi,
reduces moisture.
Cooking time approx. 2-4 hours
Calories p. portion: 140
3 portions

Quantity of ingredients:

Rice variety any 1 cup / 120g. (little) - warm - sweet.................................. metal
Water 6 cups / 700g. (yes) - cool - salty...earth

Cooking instructions:

Cook rice and water in a ratio of about 1: 6. The amount of water
determines the thickness of the mash (matter of taste).
Put the rice in a saucepan with a heavy lid. It is important to simmer the
rice after a short boil on the slightest flame, otherwise it burns.
Boil the rice for 2-4 hours. The longer it cooks, the more it strengthens.
If you want to eat the dish for breakfast, you can put the rice on just
before bedtime.
To be on the safe side, you should first check the behavior of your pot
and cooker under observation for a similar amount of time, so that
nothing burns.
Refrigerate for later use.

9.6 Basic recipe for a vegetable soup, nutritious

Strengthens spleen and lung, regulates Qi flow, builds up Qi, dries out, passes downwardly, strengthens stomach Qi.
Cooking time approx. 2-3 hours
Calories p. portion: 48
5 portions
Allergens: L

Quantity of ingredients:
Olive oil 1 table spoon / 4g. (rec.) - cool - sweet ....earth
Onion white 1 piece / 60g. (little) - warm - acrid ....metal
Carrot 3 pieces / 200g. (yes) - neutral - sweet ....earth
Parsnip 3/8 lbs - 6oz / 150g. (yes) - cool - bitter..fire
Celery root 1 cup / 100g. (rec.) - cool - sweet ....earth
Ginger fresh 1/2 teaspoon / 2g. (little) - warm - acrid ....metal
Lemon 1/2 piece / 25g. (omit) - cold - sour...wood
Juniper berry 6 pieces / 6g. (omit) - warm - sweet, acrid, bitter.....................fire
Thyme dried 1 pinch / 1g. () - warm - bitter ....metal
Lovage 1 table spoon / 3g. (omit) - warm - acrid, bitter ....metal
Bay leaf 2 leaves / 1g. () - warm - acrid..metal
Salt 1 pinch / 1g. (little) - cold - salty ....water
Water 3 cups / 650g. (yes) - cool - salty...earth

Cooking instructions:
Cut the vegetables into cubes.
Heat oil in hot pot, fry shortly onions and vegetables.
Add cold water, then add ginger, bay leaf and lemon juice.
Season with juniper, thyme and lovage. Cover for 2 - 3 hours on a low heat and simmer.
The used vegetables should be thrown away.
The basic recipe serves as a soup base and to refine vegetables, legumes or cereals.
If you want to eat vegetable soup immediately, add the desired vegetables half an hour before.
Refrigerate for later use.

9.7 Basmati rice + Zucchini tofu dish

Converts mucus, reduces heat, builds up Qi, nourishes fluids, harmonizes spleen and stomach, forces Lungen Qi.
Cooking time approx. 20 min
Calories p. portion: 146
4 portions
Allergens: E

Quantity of ingredients:

Soy Tofu 5/8 lbs - 8oz / 250g. (rec.) - cool - sweet .... earth
Olive oil 2 table spoons / 6g. (rec.) - cool - sweet .... earth
Coriander 1/2 teaspoon / 4g. (rec.) - warm - acrid .... metal
Ginger fresh 1/2 teaspoon / 4g. (little) - warm - acrid .... metal
Rice Basmati 1/2 cup / 60g. (yes) - neutral - sweet .... metal
Water 3 cups / 200g. (yes) - cool - salty .... earth
Zucchini 1 piece / 700g. (rec.) - cool - sweet .... earth

Cooking instructions:

Cut tofu cubes and marinate with olive oil, tamari, crushed coriander and ginger. Leave at least 1 hour.

Cook Basmati rice with the water. You can season with onion and cardamom.
Roast zucchini and tofu in pan in the hot oil for approx. 5-7 min.
Serve rice and tofu on a plate.
Add the parsley.

Can also be used as a salad for the home and on the go.

9.8   Breakfast - Rice with fruits

Warms the stomach and spleen, harmonizes the intestine, forces Qi, reduces moisture, preserves the fluids, contracts, nourishes fluids, moistens dryness in the lungs, produces humors, moisturizes intestines, cools inner heat.
Cooking time approx. 10 min - 3 hours
Calories p. portion: 231
3 portions
Allergens: GHO

Quantity of ingredients:

Basic recipe for a rice soup (Congee) 6 cups / 500g. (yes) - neutral - sweet ... *
Cow's milk (3.5% fat) 1/2 to 1 cup / 80g. (little) - neutral - sweet .... earth
Honey 1 table spoon / 10g. (rec.) - cold - sweet .... earth
Butter organic 1 table spoon / 15g. (rec.) - neutral - sweet .... earth
Dates dried 1 table spoon / 15g. (rec.) - warm - sweet .... earth
Fig 1 table spoon / 15g. (rec.) - warm - sweet .... earth
Apple (sour) 1 piece / 200g. (yes) - cool - sour .... wood
Hazelnuts 1/2 teaspoon / 5g. (rec.) - neutral - sweet .... earth
Almond 1/2 teaspoon / 5g. (rec.) - neutral - sweet .... earth
Cinnamon ground 1 pinch / 1g. (omit) - hot - acrid, sweet .... *

Cooking instructions:

Cook rice congee according to basic recipe or use pre-cooked.
Make it with the milk more fluid, and sweet with honey.
Fry the fruits and nuts in butter and mix with the finished rice soup, add chopped dates, figs and the apple.

9.9 Buddhist reissue soup

Nourishes blood and Qi, moisturizes lungs and stomach at Yin-emptiness, strengthens Qi and kidney Jing, moisturizes, relaxes, builds up Qi.
Cooking time approx. 2-4 hours
Calories p. portion: 280
2 portions
Allergens: G

Quantity of ingredients:

Rice variety any 1 cup / 120g. (little) - warm - sweet .... metal
Water 3 cups / 350g. (yes) - cool - salty .... earth
Butter organic 1 table spoon / 10g. (rec.) - neutral - sweet .... earth
Honey 1 teaspoon / 3g. (rec.) - cold - sweet .... earth
Cow's milk (1.5% fat) 1 cup / 120g. (little) - neutral - sweet .... earth

Cooking instructions:

Bring the rice to boil soft in the water for 2 to 4 hours. At the end of the cooking time add some milk, honey and butter. This basic recipe can be expanded as desired (sweet, salty). The indicated quantity is sufficient for 4 days (keep in a refrigerator)

Variant: The taste can be refined with cinnamon or vanilla.

9.10 Celery juice

Strengthens stomach Qi, moisturizes, relaxes, builds up Qi, spreads.
Cooking time approx. 5 min
Calories p. portion: 33
1 portion
Allergens: L

Quantity of ingredients:

Celery root 1/2 piece / 200g. (rec.) - cool - sweet .... earth
Water 1 cup / 120g. (yes) - cool - salty .... earth
Salt 1 pinch / 0,5g. (little) - cold - salty .... water

Cooking instructions:
Peel celeriac and cut into pieces and juice. Mix with water and salt as needed.

9.11 Chicken soup with angelica root and buckthorn fruit

Strengthens spleen and nourishes the blood and Yin of the liver, forces Qi and blood, is very warming.
Cooking time approx. 1 1/2 hours
Calories p. portion: 77
3 portions
Allergens: LO

Quantity of ingredients:
Basic recipe for a chicken soup (warming) 2 cup / 500g. () - warm - * .... *
Bocksdorn fruits (goji berry dried 1/8 lbs - 2oz / 50g. () - cool - .... wood

Cooking instructions:
When you cook chicken broth according to basic recipes add angelica root and willowberry fruits in the last 40 minutes.

Ingestion: Drink 2-3 cups of broth daily.

9.12 Coconut water

Nourishes Yin, blood and Jing, moisturizes, relaxes, builds up Qi, spreads.
Cooking time approx. 5 min
Calories p. portion: 30
1 portion

Quantity of ingredients:
Coconut milk 1 cup / 125g. (rec.) - warm - sweet...........................earth

Cooking instructions:
Open the coconut and strain the water.
Coconut water is also available as a ready-made drink.

9.13 Cooling rice dish with grapefruit

Lowers lung Qi, nourishes fluids, dissolves mucus, dries out, passes downwardly, warms the stomach and spleen, harmonizes the intestine, forces Qi, reduces moisture, strengthens Qi and Kidney Jing, moisturizes, relaxes, builds up Qi, spreads.
Cooking time approx. 20 min
Calories p. portion: 234
4 portions
Allergens: GHO

Quantity of ingredients:
Rice round grain 1 cup / 120g. (rec.) - neutral - sweet .... metal
Water 5 cups / 600g. (yes) - cool - salty .... earth
Hazelnuts 2 table spoons / 20g. (rec.) - neutral - sweet .... earth
Raisins 2 table spoons / 20g. (little) - warm - sweet .... earth
Agave nectar 1 table spoon / 10g. () - cool - sweet .... *
Salt 1 pinch / 0,2g. (little) - cold - salty .... water
Almond puree 1 table spoon / 10g. (rec.) - neutral - sweet........................ earth
Grapefruit (Pomelo) 1 piece / 200g. (little) - cool - sweet, sour .... fire
Butter organic 2 teaspoons / 20g. (rec.) - neutral - sweet .... earth

Cooking instructions:
Preparation on the eve: Pour round grain rice into cold water and cook. Soak chopped hazelnuts and raisins in some hot water overnight.

In the morning: Stir in a little hot water some agave syrup; add the rice and heat; add a small pinch of salt, almond paste, chopped grapefruit, the soaked chopped hazelnuts and raisins and mix; Serve with a small piece of butter.

9.14 Cous-Cous with date, coco and almondpuree

Forces Yin.
Cooking time approx. 10 min
Calories p. portion: 484
3 portions
Allergens: AHO

Quantity of ingredients:

Couscous 1 1/2 cups / 240g. (yes) - neutral - sour.................................... wood
Water 4 cups / 400g. (yes) - cool - salty... earth
Dates dried 6 pieces / 20g. (rec.) - warm - sweet...................................... earth
Coconut flakes 3 table spoons / 30g. (rec.) - warm - sweet........................ earth
Almond puree 2 table spoons / 20g. (rec.) - neutral - sweet....................... earth
Olive oil 2 teaspoons / 20g. (rec.) - cool - sweet .... earth
Apple (sweet) 1 piece grated / 120g. (rec.) - cool - sweet, sour .... earth
Vanilla 1 knife tip / 0,2g. (rec.) - neutral - sweet .... *
Chili (pod or ground) 1 pinch / 0,2g. (omit) - hot - acrid............................ metal

Cooking instructions:

Put couscous and olive oil in a large bowl and pour boiling water over them. Let it swell for 10 minutes. Crush dates and grate apple. Loosen up cous-cous with a fork. Mix in dates, coconut flakes, apple and almond paste.
Sweet to taste. Spices and flavors: vanilla, little chili

Winter variation: pear,
Summer variation: apricot, nectarine

9.15 Cucumber soup

Cools and moisturizes, diuretic, reduces damp heat, detoxifies, relaxes, builds up Qi, spreads, distributes mucus, passes downwardly, activates Wei Qi, forces Qi.
Cooking time approx. 20 min
Calories p. portion: 96
4 portions
Allergens: M

Quantity of ingredients:

Olive oil 2 table spoons / 35g. (rec.) - cool - sweet.................................... earth
Cucumber 2 pieces / 400g. (rec.) - cold - sweet.. earth
Water 2 cup / 500g. (yes) - cool - salty.. earth
Sage 3 leaves / 3g. (yes) - cool - bitter, spicy.. fire
Coriander 1 pinch / 1g. (rec.) - warm - acrid... metal
Cardamom 1 pinch / 1g. () - warm - acrid.. metal
Salt 1 pinch / 1g. (little) - cold - salty .... water

Cooking instructions:

Heat oil and roast short the small cucumbers. Add Mustard seeds, coriander, cardamom and salt. Add water. Simmer for 10-15 min. Puree and decorate with fresh chopped sage.

9.16 Curdcheesedumplings on strawberry pulp

Preserves the fluids, contracts, moisturizes the lungs, nourishes liver-blood, relaxes.
Cooking time approx. 30 min
Calories p. portion: 553
5 portions
Allergens: ACG

Quantity of ingredients:

Curd cheese 20% 1,1 lbs / 500g. (yes) - cool - sour .... wood
Spelled semolina 3/8 lbs - 6oz / 150g. (yes) - neutral - sweet .... wood
Butter organic 1/8 lbs - 2oz / 40g. (rec.) - neutral - sweet .... earth
Chicken egg 2 pieces / 120g. (rec.) - neutral - sweet .... earth
Sugar - icing sugar 2 table spoons / 20g. () - cold - sweet .... earth
Salt 1 pinch / 1g. (little) - cold - salty .... water
Breadcrumbs (bread roll) 3 table spoons / 25g. (yes) - cool - sweet, ... wood
Butter organic 10 cups / 100g. (rec.) - neutral - sweet .... earth
Strawberries 1,1 lbs / 500g. (yes) - neutral - sweet, sour .... wood
Sugar - icing sugar 3 table spoons / 25g. () - cold - sweet .... earth

Cooking instructions:

Curd-cheese, grit, butter, eggs, powdered sugar and salt to a smooth dough. Keep the dough 15 mins in the refrigerator to settle down. Then shape small dumplings with a diameter of approx. 4cm and boil them for about 10 minutes in slightly boiling salt water. Heat butter in a pan and roast the breadcrumbs golden brown. Roll the dumplings carefully into the crumbs.
Serve the dumplings with the strawberry.

9.17 Grape juice with hot water

Cooking time approx. 5 min
Calories p. portion: 44
2 portions
Allergens:
Quantity of ingredients:

Grape juice red 1 cup / 120g. (rec.) - neutral - sweet, sour .... earth
Water 1 cup / 120g. (yes) - cool - salty .... earth

Cooking instructions:

Add grape juice to hot water.

9.18 Hungarian rice salad

Warms the stomach and spleen, harmonizes the intestine, forces Qi, reduces moisture, helps to digest fat, supports the urination, reduces blood pressure.
Cooking time approx. 25 min
Calories p. portion: 421
2 portions
Allergens: GM

Quantity of ingredients:

Rice (whole grain) 1/2 cup / 60g. (little) - warm - sweet............................. metal
Water 3 cups / 300g. (yes) - cool - salty .... earth
Salt 1 pinch / 0,3g. (little) - cold - salty .... water
Tomato 1/4 lbs - 4oz / 100g. (little) - cold - sweet-sour .... wood
Peppers 1/8 lbs - 2oz / 50g. (little) - cool - sweet .... earth
Champignon 1 oz / 30g. (rec.) - cool - sweet.. earth
Edam cheese 1 oz / 30g. () - neutral - sweet.. earth
Yogurt (natural, 1.5% fat) 1/8 lbs - 2oz / 45g. (little) - cool - sour .... wood
Salt 1 pinch / 1g. (little) - cold - salty .... water
Rapeseed oil 2 table spoons / 20g. (rec.) - neutral - sweet......................... earth
Pepper (ground) 1 pinch / 0,2g. () - warm - acrid .... metal

Cooking instructions:

Pour the rice into plenty of boiling salt water and let it drain gently. Wash tomatoes and peppers and core. Cut both in to small cubes. Peel the mushrooms (from the tin or with rapeseed oil for a short time) and cut the cheese into small cubes and add to the rice. Prepare the marinade and mix with the ingredients, refrigerate and leave for at least an hour.

9.19 Italian champignon rice

Nourishes blood, moisturizes, relaxes, builds up Qi, spreads, wearms the stomach and spleen, harmonizes the intestine, forces Qi, reduces moisture, directs upwards, moisturizes, relaxes, builds up Qi, spreads.
Cooking time approx. 25 min
Calories p. portion: 256
4 portions
Allergens: G

Quantity of ingredients:

Rice round grain 1 1/2 cups / 240g. (rec.) - neutral - sweet........................ metal
Water 2 cup / 450g. (yes) - cool - salty..earth
Pepper (ground) 1 pinch / 0,2g. () - warm - acrid .... metal
Salt 1 pinch / 0,5g. (little) - cold - salty .... water
Lemon juice 1 dash / 2g. (omit) - cold - sour .... wood
Champignon 5/8 lbs - 8oz / 250g. (rec.) - cool - sweet..............................earth
Pepper powder (hot) 1 pinch / 0,2g. () - warm - bitter...................................fire
Olive oil 1 teaspoon / 3g. (rec.) - cool - sweet ....earth
Chives 1 teaspoon / 5g. (little) - warm - acrid .... metal

Cooking instructions:
Put the round grain rice in cold water 1:6 and cook.
Add ground pepper, salt, plenty of lemon juice, rose paprika, a little olive oil or butter and mix well.
Carefully add in mushrooms, chives or the green parts of the spring onion, and carefully add in some grated Parmesan cheese.
Goes well with vegetables and tofu dishes, tomato sauce dishes.

9.20 Kohlrabi Potatoes mash

Moves Qi and blood, reduces moisture, forces Qi, forces spleen, relieves inflammation, moisturizes, relaxes, builds up Qi, spreads, forces kidney Jing.
Cooking time approx. 25 min
Calories p. portion: 278
1 portion
Allergens: CG

Quantity of ingredients:
Kohlrabi 1/2 piece / 150g. (rec.) - neutral - acrid, sweet.............................earth
Potato 1/4 lbs - 4oz / 100g. (rec.) - neutral - sweet ....earth
Potato 10 cups / 100g. (rec.) - neutral - sweet ....earth
Butter organic 1 table spoon / 10g. (rec.) - neutral - sweet.........................earth
Chicken yolk 1 piece / 25g. (rec.) - neutral - sweet ....earth

Cooking instructions:
Remove the kohlrabi leaves, wash the tuber and tender leaves and the potatoes thoroughly. Peel the kohlrabi and potatoes, cut into cubes about 1 cm in size. Melt half the butter in a small saucepan, add the kohlrabi and the potatoes and fry in it. Steam with 2 tablespoons of water in a closed saucepan over low heat for about 15 minutes. Meanwhile, free the tenderest kohlrabi leaves from the stems and chop very finely. In total, at most 2 tablespoons of leaf pieces should be used. Add this to the vegetables about 5 minutes before the end of the cooking time. Stir in the egg yolk and bring to the boil again. Put the

vegetables in a plate and mix with the remaining butter and egg yolk. (Crush for the baby with a fork.)

9.21 Milk-free cereal fruit porridge

Nourishes fluids, reduces stomach heat, harmonizes stomach, strengthens Qi, produces body fluids, strengthens
spleen and stomach.
Cooking time approx. 10 min
Calories p. portion: 220
1 portion
Allergens: AG

Quantity of ingredients:
Apple (sweet) 1 piece / 100g. (rec.) - cool - sweet, sour ....earth
Strawberries 3 pieces / 15g. (yes) - neutral - sweet, sour .... wood
Water 1/2 cup / 100g. (yes) - cool - salty...earth
Oat flakes (whole grain) 1/2 oz / 20g. (little) - warm - sweet......................metal
Butter organic 1 table spoon / 10g. (rec.) - neutral - sweet.........................earth

Cooking instructions:
Wash the apple thoroughly, peel with a peeler and grate finely on an apple grater. Wash the strawberries, peel off the green and crush the berries very finely with a fork. Heat the water till it boils. Fill the flakes into a plate, pour boiling water and stir well. Then add the butter and undergo. Finally, add the grated apple and strawberries.

9.22 Millet with egg and butter

Forces blood, Yin and Jing, nourishes Yin, moisturizes in case of internal dryness, forces blood, forces spleen, calms nerves and stomach, strengthens spleen and kidney, diuretic, strengthens Qi and kidney Jing, moisturizes, relaxes, builds up Qi, spreads
Cooking time approx. 25 min
Calories p. portion: 338
2 portions
Allergens: CG

Quantity of ingredients:
Millet 1 cup / 100g. (rec.) - cool - sweet, salty ....earth
Ginger fresh 1/2 teaspoon / 1g. (little) - warm - acrid .... metal
Salt 1 pinch / 0,5g. (little) - cold - salty .... water
Parsley 2 table spoons / 16g. (omit) - warm - bitter.................................... wood
Pepper powder (hot) 1 pinch / 1g. () - warm - bitter..fire
Chicken egg 2 pieces / 100g. (rec.) - neutral - sweet ....earth

Butter organic 2 table spoons / 20g. (rec.) - neutral - sweet........................earth
Nutmeg 1 pinch / 0,2g. (omit) - warm - acrid .... metal
Water 1 1/2 cups / 200g. (yes) - cool - salty..earth

Cooking instructions:
Simmer the millet with the ginger and nutmeg in the water for 5 min.
and let it swell for another 30 min.
Cook and peel 1 soft egg per person; pile up the millet on plates and
place 1 egg each in a hollow in the millet mountain; Put butter flakes
over it. Sprinkle with chopped parsley and the rose paprika.

9.23 Miso soup with tofu

Nourish the humors, preserves the fluids, contracts, nourishes fluids,
lets Qi ascend, harmonizes spleen and stomach, moisturizes, relaxes,
builds up Qi, spreads, regulates Qi, warms spleen and kidney, dissolves
stagnation, directs upwards.
Cooking time approx. 5 min
Calories p. portion: 51
3 portions
Allergens: E

Quantity of ingredients:
Wakame 1 piece / 5g. (yes) - cold - salty ....water
Miso 3-4 table spoons / 30g. () - neutral - salty ....water
Soy Tofu 1/8 lbs - 2oz / 50g. (rec.) - cool - sweet......................................earth
Water 2 cup / 500g. (yes) - cool - salty..earth
Soy sauce 1 dash / 3g. (little) - cold - salty...water
Onion (spring onion) 1/2 teaspoon / 6g. (little) - warm - acrid.................... metal

Cooking instructions:
Boil soybean seedlings, wakame algae and diced tofu for 5 minutes.
Put the miso paste in the soup plate and slowly pour over the soup.
Season with Tamari sauce. Sprinkle with cutted spring onion.

9.24 Oyster mushrooms with asparagus

Tonifies lungs and kidneys Yin, balances heat, dissipates moisture.
Cooking time approx. 30 min
Calories p. portion: 316
4 portions
Allergens: GH

Quantity of ingredients:
Onion white 1 piece / 50g. (little) - warm - acrid .... metal
Butter organic 2 table spoons / 40g. (rec.) - neutral - sweet....................... earth
Oyster mushroom 3/4 lbs / 300g. (rec.) - neutral - sweet .... earth
Sake 2 table spoons / 40g. (omit) - warm - sweet, bitter, acrid................. metal
Parsley 2 table spoons / 40g. (omit) - warm - bitter.................................. wood
Walnuts 3 table spoons / 60g. (little) - warm - sweet................................. earth
Asparagus (green or white) 1,1 lbs / 500g. (rec.) - cool - sweet, bitter .... earth
Salt 1 pinch / 1g. (little) - cold - salty .... water
Sugar white 1 pinch / 0,1g. (little) - cold - sweet..................................... earth
Potato 1 lbs / 500g. (rec.) - neutral - sweet .... earth

Cooking instructions:
Cook organically grown potatoes with the skin, otherwise prepare
peeled boiled potatoes. Boil the asparagus in salted water with a pinch
of sugar and salt. (You can cook an old roll that absorbs the bittering
substances.) Slightly sauté the chopped onions in a pan in the butter
before frying the oyster mushrooms cut into the same pan. Stew 15
minutes, stirring several times. Add the sake, walnuts and parsley and
simmer on low heat while you drain the potatoes and asparagus.
Finally, sprinkle some herbal salt over it.
If no fresh asparagus is available, asparagus can be used in jars.

9.25 Pear compote

Moisturizes lungs, reduces lung mucus, nourishes lungs Qi.
Cooking time approx. 20 min
Calories p. portion: 100
3 portions

Quantity of ingredients:
Water 1 1/2 cups / 240g. (yes) - cool - salty .... earth
Pear 4 pieces / 500g. (rec.) - cool - sweet, sour.. earth

Cooking instructions:
Halve organic pears. Cores and skin can be used. Pear in the pot and
add water. Simmer for up to 20 minutes until pears are tender.

9.26 Pear juice

Moisturizes lungs, reduces lung mucus, nourishes lungs Qi.
Cooking time approx. 5 min
Calories p. portion: 180
2 portions

Quantity of ingredients:
Pear 3 pieces / 600g. (rec.) - cool - sweet, sour..earth

Cooking instructions:
Peel pears thinly (vitamins under the skin) and core. Juice in the juicer.

9.27 Radish with sugar

Nourishes the lungs and spleen, distributes mucus, dissolves mucus, dissolves stagnation, directs upwards, warms the three-heater, relieves weakness.
Cooking time approx. 5 min
Calories p. portion: 46
2 portions

Quantity of ingredients:
Radish (white, green…) 1 piece / 400g. (rec.) - cool - sweet, acrid...........metal
Sugar brown 1 teaspoon / 4g. (little) - warm - sweet ....earth

Cooking instructions:
Grate the radish and sprinkle with sugar.

9.28 Radishjuice

Nourishes the lungs and spleen, distributes mucus, Dissolves mucus, dissolves stagnation, directs upwards.
Cooking time approx. 10 min
Calories p. portion: 9
1 portion

Quantity of ingredients:
Radish (white, green…) 1/2 piece / 50g. (rec.) - cool - sweet, acrid..........metal
Water 1 cup / 120g. (yes) - cool - salty...earth

Cooking instructions:
Make the radish juice with the juicer or buy it at the food store.
The fresh press juice is extracted from the root.
For healing purpose prefer the black radish because of its sharpness.
The pungent taste is due to the mustard oils in the radish juice.
They stimulate bile-juice production in the liver. This has two different effects in our body. The appetite and digestion are promoted and alleviates bile and liver disease.
Drink in small sips.

9.29 Red lentils with avocado and radish

Nutritious and moisturizing builds up Qi and fluids, drives sweat, reduces blood fat, stimulates, dissolves stagnation.
Cooking time approx. 20 min
Calories p. portion: 269
3 portions
Allergens: N

Quantity of ingredients:
Ginger fresh 2 slices / 2g. (little) - warm - acrid .... metal
Water 1 1/2 cups / 200g. (yes) - cool - salty .... earth
Lentils red 1 cup peeled / 100g. (yes) - neutral - salty.............................. water
Wakame 1 inch / 1g. (yes) - cold - salty .... water
Salt 1 pinch / 0,5g. (little) - cold - salty .... water
Lemon juice 1 splash / 1g. (omit) - cold - sour.. wood
Turmeric (yellow root) 1 pinch / 0,3g. (little) - warm - bitter .... *
Avocado 1 piece / 300g. (rec.) - cold - sweet .... earth
Pepper (ground) 1 pinch / 0,2g. () - warm - acrid .... metal
Sesame oil 1 dash / 1g. (rec.) - cool - sweet .... earth
Radish (white, green…) 1 cup / 100g. (rec.) - cool - sweet, acrid.............. metal

Cooking instructions:
Put in a pot with water, some chopped ginger, peeled red lentils, a piece of wakame or a small amount of hijiki and simmer until the lentils are soft. Season with salt, lemon juice and turmeric.
Meanwhile: place half an avocado per serving on one-third of the plate: add ground pepper, a pinch of salt, a little lemon juice, a pinch of sweet pepper and a little sesame oil.
Put the grated radish on the second plate third.
Fill the lentil dish into the last third of the plate.
Variant: Use radish slices instead of radishes.

9.30 Reissue soup with duck

Nourishes Yin, warms the stomach and spleen, harmonizes the intestine, forces Qi, reduces moisture, nourishes blood and liver, harmonizes liver and spleen, moisturizes, relaxes, builds up Qi, spreads.
Cooking time approx. 1 1/2 hours
Calories p. portion: 161
6 portions
Allergens: EG

Quantity of ingredients:
Rice round grain 1 cup / 100g. (rec.) - neutral - sweet .... metal
Water 8 cups / 900g. (yes) - cool - salty .... earth
Duck (slaughtered) 5/8 lbs - 8oz / 250g. (rec.) - cool - sweet, salty .... wood
Shiitake, dried 4-6 pieces / 5g. (rec.) - neutral - sweet .... earth
Parsley 2 table spoons / 12g. (omit) - warm - bitter .... wood
Butter organic 1 teaspoon / 3g. (rec.) - neutral - sweet .... earth
Soy sauce 1 dash / 2g. (little) - cold - salty .... water

Cooking instructions:
Soak shiitake mushrooms. Prepare rice soup according to the basic recipe. Add duck meat and shiitake mushrooms
for the last 30 minutes. Add oyster mushrooms, parsley and a little butter at the very end. Season with soy sauce.

Variant: Add soaked and cooked adzuki beans. They enhance the diuretic effect.

9.31 Rice congee with honey pear and black sesame

Especially good in kidney Yin deficiency, moisturizes lungs, cools heat, reduces lung mucus, produces humors, moisturizes, relaxes, builds up Qi, spreads, moisturizes intestines, nourishes Yin.
Cooking time approx. 10 min - 3 hours
Calories p. portion: 158
2 portions
Allergens: N

Quantity of ingredients:
Basic recipe ... (Congee) 1 1/2 cups / 240g. (yes) - neutral - sweet .... *
Pear 2 pieces / 300g. (rec.) - cool - sweet, sour .... earth

Cooking instructions:

Cook rice congee according to basic recipe.

Fill pot with 3 cm of water and heat till it boils. Quarter the pears (with the skin and seeds) and simmer them covered with black sesame for 10 minutes. Mix with the rice.

9.32 Rice with stewed vegetables

Dissipates heat and moisture.
Cooking time approx. 20 min
Calories p. portion: 166
2 portions
Allergens: L

Quantity of ingredients:

Rice variety any 1/2 cup / 60g. (little) - warm - sweet................................ metal
Water 3 cups / 300g. (yes) - cool - salty .... earth
Lemon peel 1 piece / 3g. (yes) - cool - bitter .... fire
Water 1/2 cup / 0g. (yes) - cool - salty.. earth
Carrot 2 pieces / 180g. (yes) - neutral - sweet .... earth
Celery sticks 1/2 piece / 5g. (rec.) - cool - sweet .... earth
Champignon 1/2 cup / 50g. (rec.) - cool - sweet.. earth
Cress 2 table spoons / 20g. (rec.) - cool - sweet .... metal
Linseed oil 1 dash / 3g. () - neutral - sweet .... earth

Cooking instructions:

Cook rice according to basic recipe with a piece of lemon peel.
Steam chopped carrots, celery and mushrooms until soft.
Then sprinkle with cress. Then add a dash of high quality cold oil.

9.33 Roasted millet with Celery sticks

Strengthens spleen and kidney, diuretic, brings the liver Qi in motion, cools heat, moisturizes, relaxes, builds up Qi, spreads.
Cooking time approx. 30 min
Calories p. portion: 400
2 portions
Allergens: L

Quantity of ingredients:
Millet 1 cup / 120g. (rec.) - cool - sweet, salty ....earth
Water 1 1/2 cups / 240g. (yes) - cool - salty..earth
Celery sticks 2 rods / 50g. (rec.) - cool - sweet ....earth
Water 2 table spoons / 30g. (yes) - cool - salty ....earth
Salt 1 pinch / 1g. (little) - cold - salty .... water
Sage 3-4 leaves / 2g. (yes) - cool - bitter, spicy ....fire
Cress 1 teaspoon / 3g. (rec.) - cool - sweet.. metal

Cooking instructions:
Roast millet briefly, pour over water, heat till it boils and let stand for 20
min. to swell.
Cut celery into small pieces and mix with water, salt and fresh herbs
and cook for 10 min. Add to the millet. Sprinkle fresh sage or
watercress over it.

9.34 Roasted nuts

Strengthens kidney Qi, essence and brain, forces kidney, builds up
essence, warms lungs, moistens the intestine, moisturizes, relaxes,
builds up Qi, spreads.
Cooking time approx. 5 min
Calories p. portion: 973
2 portions
Allergens: H

Quantity of ingredients:
Hazelnuts 1/4 lbs - 4oz / 100g. (rec.) - neutral - sweet...............................earth
Cashews 10 cups / 100g. (rec.) - cool - sweet ....earth
Walnuts 1/4 lbs - 4oz / 100g. (little) - warm - sweet....................................earth

Cooking instructions:
Roast nuts in a pan for about 5 minutes.

9.35 Semolina slices

Nourishes fluids, moisturizes dryness, produces humors, moisturizes
intestines, cools inner heat, builds up Qi, spreads, moisturizes,
preserves the fluids, contracts.
Cooking time approx. 30 min
Calories p. portion: 331
1 portion
Allergens: AG

Quantity of ingredients:
Cow's milk (3.5% fat) 3/4 cup - 6 oz / 200g. (little) - neutral - sweet..........earth
Wheat semolina 1 oz / 30g. (yes) - cool - sweet, salty .... wood
Butter organic 1 teaspoon / 3g. (rec.) - neutral - sweet ....earth
Banana 3 oz / 80g. (little) - cool - sweet, rough ....earth
Orange juice 1 teaspoon / 3g. (little) - cold - sour, sweet .... wood

Cooking instructions:
Preheat the oven to 200°C/392°F (gas level 3). Heat 125 ml. of milk till it boils and let the semolina trickle in. Cook over medium heat. Stir in the butter. Spread the porridge in a ragout fin-frying pan, bake in the oven (center) in light brown for about 15 minutes. Puree the remaining milk with the banana and the orange juice and pour everything into a deep dish. Remove the porridge, cut into slices and place next to the sauce.

9.36 Spelled-grid porridge with berries of the season

Nourishes fluids, moisturizes dryness, produces humors, moisturizes intestines, cools inner heat, preserves the fluids, contracts, forces middle, nourishes heart and liver-blood, preserves the fluids, contracts.
Cooking time approx. 15 min
Calories p. portion: 244
2 portions
Allergens: AGH

Quantity of ingredients:
Cow's milk (1.5% fat) 1/2 cup / 125g. (little) - neutral - sweet.....................earth
Water 1/2 cup / 125g. (yes) - cool - salty...earth
Spelled semolina 5 table spoons / 50g. (yes) - neutral - sweet .... wood
Butter organic 2 teaspoons / 20g. (rec.) - neutral - sweet ....earth
Berries of the season 10 cups / 100g. () - neutral - sweet, sour .... wood
Honey 1-2 teaspoons / 5g. (rec.) - cold - sweet...earth
Almond 1-2 teaspoons / 5g. (rec.) - neutral - sweet ....earth
Peppermint 3-4 leaves / 2g. (rec.) - cool - acrid, bitter .... metal
Cinnamon ground 1 pinch / 0,5g. (omit) - hot - acrid, sweet............................. *
Vanilla 1 pinch / 0,2g. (rec.) - neutral - sweet... *
Cocoa 1 pinch / 0,5g. (omit) - warm - sweet, bitter..fire
Coconut grated 1 table spoon / 10g. (rec.) - warm - sweet..........................earth

Cooking instructions:
Stir in spelled semolina in cold water and boil slowly over medium heat. After boiling, remove from the heat and let
simmer for a few minutes. Depending on the desired consistency, some water may have to be added. Stir in the butter and fine grated nuts in the mash and raspberries. Serve with honey or whole-grain sugar as

desired.
Spices and aromas: fresh mint, cinnamon or vanilla, cocoa, coconut

Summer: raspberries, blueberries, strawberries

9.37 Spring vegetables

Cools heat, diuretic, cools blood, reduces mucus, moisturizes, relaxes, builds Qi, distributes, strengthen the middle, nourishes lung Yin, produces humors.
Cooking time approx. 1 1/2 hour
Calories p. portion: 64
8 portions
Allergens: G

Quantity of ingredients:
Carrot 1,1 lbs / 500g. (yes) - neutral - sweet ....earth
Kohlrabi 1,1 lbs / 500g. (rec.) - neutral - acrid, sweet..................................earth
Butter organic 2 table spoons / 20g. (rec.) - neutral - sweet.......................earth
Water 1/2 cup / 125g. (yes) - cool - salty..earth

Cooking instructions:
Wash the vegetables thoroughly. Clean and peel carrots and turnip cabbage. From the turnip cabbage, finely chop some delicate leaves and set aside. Rasp the carrots and the turnip cabbage. Melt the butter, add the water and the vegetables and cook over medium heat for about 30 minutes. Stir occasionally. Spread the vegetables and cooked water to about 8 deep-frozen bags to a100-150 g (depending on the age of the child). Close the bags, allow them to cool down and freeze them for max 3 months.
If necessary thaw, boil and mix with 80g of boiled potatoes and an egg. (The recipe can easily be varied if you want to use cauliflower, peas or zucchini)

9.38 Tea from celery sticks

Brings the Liver Qi in motion, cools heat, moisturizes, relaxes, builds up Qi, spreads.
Cooking time approx. 15 min
Calories p. portion: 1
4 portions
Allergens: L

Quantity of ingredients:

Celery sticks 2 table spoons (chopped) / 18g. (rec.) - cool - sweet ....earth
Water 2 cup / 500g. (yes) - cool - salty...earth

Cooking instructions:

Heat the water till it boils and put it aside. Add cutted celery and cook for 10 min. to let go. Strain. Sweet to taste with honey.

9.39 Tea from chamomile

Reduces internal wind and heat, cools liver.
Cooking time approx. 10 min
Calories p. portion: 0
1 portion

Quantity of ingredients:

Chamomile 1 teaspoon / 3g. () - cool - sweet, bitter..............................*
Water 1 cup / 120g. (yes) - cool - salty...earth

Cooking instructions:

Heat the water till it boils and put it aside. Chamomile flowers added and 10 min. to let go.

9.40 Tea from coriander

Sudorific, reduces wind.
Cooking time approx. 10 min
Calories p. portion: 2
4 portions

Quantity of ingredients:

Coriander 1 teaspoon / 3g. (rec.) - warm - acrid..metal
Water 2 cup / 500g. (yes) - cool - salty...earth

Cooking instructions:

Heat the water till it boils and put it aside. Add coriander and 10 min. to let go. Sweet to taste with honey. Strain when pouring.

9.41 Tea from peppermint with white sugar

Cools heat, distributes mucus, derives wind-cold and wind-heat, brings the stomach Qi in motion, solves congestion, forces Qi, moisturizes lungs.
Cooking time approx. 15 min
Calories p. portion: 8
2 portions

Quantity of ingredients:
Peppermint 1 table spoon / 7g. (rec.) - cool - acrid, bitter .... metal
Water 2 cup / 500g. (yes) - cool - salty.. earth
Sugar candy white 1 teaspoon / 3g. (rec.) - neutral - sweet .... earth

Cooking instructions:
Heat the water till it boils and put it aside. Add peppermint and 10 min. to let go. Strain. Sweet to taste with honey.

9.42 Tea from red dates

Nourishes blood, promotes the build-up of Qi and blood, moisturizes lungs, produces humors, strengthens spleen and stomach.
Cooking time approx. 10 min
Calories p. portion: 12
4 portions
Allergens: O

Quantity of ingredients:
Dates dried 2-4 pieces / 15g. (rec.) - warm - sweet................................... earth
Water 2 cup / 500g. (yes) - cool - salty.. earth

Cooking instructions:
Heat the water till it boils and put it aside. Add chopped dates and 10 min. to let go. Sweet to taste with honey. Strain when pouring.

9.43 Tsampa with jam or fruit compote

Nourishes fluids, reduces stomach heat, forces spleen, produces essence, harmonizes stomach, moisturizes intestines.
Cooking time approx. 5 min
Calories p. portion: 280
1 portion
Allergens: AGO

Quantity of ingredients:

Tsampa 3 table spoons / 30g. (rec.) - cold - sweet, little salty ....earth
Water 6-8 table spoons / 70g. (yes) - cool - salty ....earth
Butter organic 1/2 teaspoon / 2g. (rec.) - neutral - sweet ....earth
Strawberry jam 1 table spoon / 7g. () - neutral - sweet, sour.....................wood
Sunflower seeds 2 teaspoons / 14g. (rec.) - neutral - sweet ....earth
Apple (sweet) 1 piece grated / 120g. (rec.) - cool - sweet, sour ....earth

Cooking instructions:

Pour Tsampa (roasted barley flour) with boiling water and stir with a
spoon until a porridge is formed.
Add butter, jam, sunflower seeds and grated apple.
Sweet to taste with honey, whole cane sugar, or barley malt.
Spices and herbs: fresh mint, vanilla or cocoa, anise, cinnamon.

Summer: jam or compote of your choice
Winter: nuts and apple or pear

9.44 Vegetable miso soup with tofu

Strengthens spleen and liver, regulates Qi flow, moisturizes, relaxes,
builds up Qi, spreads, forces Qi, forces liver and kidney, reduces damp
heat, detoxifies, nourishes fluids, reduces internal heat, dries out,
passes downwardly.
Cooking time approx. 15 min
Calories p. portion: 107
4 portions
Allergens: EN

Quantity of ingredients:

Sesame oil 2 table spoons / 35g. (rec.) - cool - sweet................................earth
Onion (shallot) 1 piece / 20g. (little) - warm - acrid, sweet.........................metal
Carrot 1 piece / 70g. (yes) - neutral - sweet ....earth
Leek 2 inches / 10g. (little) - warm - acrid...metal
Water 3 cups / 750g. (yes) - cool - salty ....earth
Endive salad 2 table spoons / 30g. (yes) - neutral - bitter ....fire
Soy Tofu 2 table spoons / 30g. (rec.) - cool - sweet ....earth
Ginger fresh 1/2 teaspoon / 1g. (little) - warm - acrid ....metal
Miso 2 table spoons / 15g. () - neutral - salty ....water

Cooking instructions:

In sesame oil first sauté onions, then carrots and a little leek; Pour in
water and simmer gently; add the bean sprouts and endive leaves and
leave to stand; Tofu cubes, add a little ginger; at the end stir in a little
cooled cooking-water the Miso.

9.45 Vegetable potato and meat mash

Strengthens spleen and liver, regulates Qi flow, moisturizes, relaxes, builds up Qi.
Cooking time approx. 30 min
Calories p. portion: 127
2 portions

Quantity of ingredients:
Potato 10 cups / 100g. (rec.) - neutral - sweet ....earth
Carrot (Early Carrot) 5/8 oz / 200g. (yes) - neutral - sweet.........................earth
Beef meat (calf) 1/8 lbs - 2oz / 40g. (rec.) - neutral - sweet.........................earth
Apricots juice 6 table spoons / 60g. () - warm - sweet.................................earth
Rapeseed oil 1 table spoon / 6g. (rec.) - neutral - sweet.............................earth

Cooking instructions:
Remove the flesh, skin, tendons and grease, wash under cool water and cut into small pieces and boil in a little water. After about 15-20 minutes, remove and puree. Wash the vegetables and potatoes, peel and cut into not too small pieces. Cook gently with a little water over a low heat for 10-20 minutes. Use the blender to chop the vegetables. Mix everything, add butter or oil and fruit juice and puree again.

Alternately use other meats such as chicken, lamb or turkey. Also change vegetables with zucchini, kohlrabi, fennel, pumpkin, parsnips and broccoli.

Also change the fruit juices. This can produce a variety of flavors.

9.46 Vegetarian vegetable-oatmeal-potatoes mash

Forces Qi, forces spleen, relieves inflammation, moisturizes, relaxes, builds up Qi, spreads, cools heat, nourishes fluids.
Cooking time approx. 25 min
Calories p. portion: 91
2 portions
Allergens: A

Quantity of ingredients:
Carrot (Early Carrot) 1 oz / 30g. (yes) - neutral - sweet ....earth
Parsnip 1 oz / 30g. (yes) - cool - bitter...fire
Zucchini 1 oz / 30g. (rec.) - cool - sweet..earth
Fennel 1/2 oz / 10g. (little) - warm - sweet, little acrid ....earth
Potato 1/8 lbs - 2oz / 50g. (rec.) - neutral - sweet ....earth
Water 1/2 oz / 20g. (yes) - cool - salty...earth

Oat flakes (whole grain) 1/2 oz / 10g. (little) - warm - sweet......................metal
Orange juice 1 oz / 30g. (little) - cold - sour, sweet ....wood
Rapeseed oil 1/4 oz / 8g. (rec.) - neutral - sweet..earth

Cooking instructions:
Wash the vegetables and potatoes, dice and fry in a little water. Add water and oatmeal, puree everything and finally add the oil. Note: This porridge replaces the vegetable-potato-meat porridge when meat is to be dispensed with in the infant's diet. Since meat is the best food source for iron, a vegetarian diet must pay particular attention to a sufficient supply of iron.

9.47 Wheat fresh grain porridge with pears.

Moisturizes lungs, cools heat, reduces lung mucus, nourishes Yin from heart and kidney, forces heart and kidney, moisturizes, relaxes, builds up Qi, spreads.
Cooking time approx. 25 min
Calories p. portion: 309
2 portions
Allergens: ANO

Quantity of ingredients:
Wheat 1 cup / 100g. (yes) - cool - sweet..wood
Water 2-4 cups / 350g. (yes) - cool - salty..earth
Pear 2 pieces / 300g. (rec.) - cool - sweet, sour...earth
Raisins 1 table spoon / 10g. (little) - warm - sweet......................................earth
Sesame, white 1 table spoon / 8g. () - neutral - sweet ....earth
Sunflower seeds 1 table spoon / 8g. (rec.) - neutral - sweet ....earth
Cardamom 1 pinch / 0,3g. () - warm - acrid..metal
Salt 1 pinch / 0,3g. (little) - cold - salty ....water

Cooking instructions:
Preparation the night before: Wheat roughly cut; soak overnight.

In the morning: Put the wheat meal with a little hot water; simmer with stirring for about 15 minutes.
Meanwhile, add pear compote, raisins, crushed sesame, sunflower seeds, some ground cardamom, a small pinch of salt.

Variants: with grated apple or seasonal fruit.

10 Effects of food

10.1 Use ingredients: recommendable

Almond
Almond marzipan
Almond milk
Almond puree
Apple (sweet)
Apple juice (natural cloudy)
Arrowroot
Asparagus (green or white)
Avocado
Barley
Barley malt
Barley not peeled
Beef meat (calf)
Boletus mushroom
Broad beans (thick beans)
Broccoli
Brussels sprouts
Buckwheat
Butter organic
Calamari
Cantaloupe
Cashews
Cauliflower
Celery root
Celery sticks
Champignon
Chanterelle
Chicken egg
Chicken stomach
Chicken yolk
Chickpeas
Chinese cabbage
Coconut flakes
Coconut grated
Coconut milk
Coriander
Corn
Corn Grease (Polenta)
Cress
Crucian
Cucumber
Dates dried
Dill
Duck (heart)
Duck (slaughtered)
Fig
Fig dried
Fresh cheese
Freshwater fish

Goose
Goose parts
Gourd
Grape juice red
Grape juice white
Grapes red
Hazelnuts
Hibiscus
Honey
Iceberg lettuce
Kohlrabi
Malt
Maple syrup
Margarine
Margarine (diet)
Millet
Millet flakes
Morel (black, dried)
Morel, dried
Mung bean sprouting
Olive oil
Oyster mushroom
Oysters
Peanut oil
Peanuts
Pear
Peas, green
Peppermint
Perch
Pine nuts
Pistachios
Pork heart
Pork knuckle
Pork meat
Pork skin
Potato
Pumpkin
Pumpkin seeds
Quail egg
Quince
Rabbit
Rabbit meat
Radish (white, green, purple-red)
Rapeseed oil
Red cabbage
Reishi mushroom
Rice long grain rice
Rice round grain
Rice wild (nature rice)

Saffron
Salsify
Sesame oil
Sesame paste (Tahini)
Shiitake, dried
Soy Tofu
Soybean milk
Soybeans, black
Sugar candy white
Sugar cane sugar
Sugar fructose - fruit sugar
Sugar glucose - grapes sugar
Sugar Milk Sugar

Sunflower oil
Sunflower seeds
Sweet potato
Tarragon (Estragon)
Trout
Tsampa (roasted barley flour)
Umeboshi plums (Japanese apricots)
Vanilla
Vanilla powder
Vegetable juice
Wheat germ oil
White beans
Zucchini

10.2 Use ingredients: yes

Adzuki beans
Apple (sour)
Artichoke
Balm
Basic recipe for a rice soup (Congee)
Beef liver
Beer (Pils)
Beer (Top-fermented German dark beer)
Blackberry´s
Black-eyed peas
Blueberry
Blueberry juice
Breadcrumbs (wheat bread, bread roll)
Bulgur (cereals)
Buttermilk
Carp
Carrot
Carrot (Early Carrot)
Carrot juice without sugar
Chicory
Chlorella (fresh water)
Clementines
Coix (seeds) YiYi Ren
Couscous
Cranberry
Cranberry juice
Cream, sweet 30%
Curd cheese 20%
Curd cheese 40%
Currant (black)
Currant (red)
Currant (white)
Elderberry blossom tee
Endive salad
Fish pieces mixed (fresh water)
Gooseberry
Grapes white

Ground
Ground caraway
Hawthorn
Herbs different varieties
Herbs various
Kefir
Kombu seaweed (Saccharina japonica)
Lemon peel
Lentils
Lentils black
Lentils red
Lentils yellow
Lettuce
Lychee
Lychee in Preserved
Mallow (Malva sylvestris) blossom tea
Multi-grain bread (gray bread)
Mung bean
Octopus
Olives
Parsnip
Pear juice
Peas
Pigeon
Pineapple
Pineapple juice without sugar
Quail
Quinoa
Radicchio
Radish black
Raspberry
Raspberry dried (immature)
Rice (Gaoliang / Sorghum)
Rice Basmati
Rice mash
Rice noodles
Rice sticky
Romaine lettuce / lettuce salad

Rye
Rye flour
Sage
Salmon
Sauerkraut (cutted cabbage fermented)
Shark
Sour cherries
Sour cream (Schmand) 30% fat
Sour cream 15% fat
Sour milk
Soybeans, yellow
Spelled (Dark) bread
Spelled grain
Spelled semolina

Spelled wholemeal flour
Strawberries
Strawberry Juice
Tangerine
Wakame
Water
Water hot
Wheat
Wheat bulgur
Wheat flakes
Wheat flour
Wheat semolina
Wheat semolina for children
White bread (wheat bread)

10.3 Use ingredients: little

Agar agar (kelp)
Amaranth
Anchovy / Sardine
Anise (Common Fennel)
Apricot
Apricots
Aubergine
Bamboo shoots
Banana
Banana (cooking banana)
Bean oil
Beef fillet
Beef meat
Beef meatbones
Beef stomach
Bitter melon
Burdock root tea
Carambola (Star fruit)
Caviar
Chard
Cherry
Cherry juice
Chestnuts
Chicken meat
Chives
Clove
Cod
Cow's milk (1.5% fat)
Cow's milk (whole milk 3.5% fat)
Crab
Cumin (Caraway seed)
Dandelion (young plants)
Dandelionroots tea
Deer meat
Deer meat
Eel

Fennel
Fennel tea
French beans
Ginger fresh
Goose egg
Grapefruit (Pomelo)
Grapefruit juice
Grass carp
Green spelt
Kiwi
Kumquats
Lady's mantle
Lamb's lettuce
Leek
Lime
Lobster
Longane
Mango
mango powder
Marjoram
Miso paste (soy bean paste)
Mozzarella
Mulberry fruit
Mullet
Mussels
Mustard seeds
Oat
Oat flakes (whole grain)
Oat flour
Oat fusion (baby food)
Oat meal
Okra
Onion (shallot)
Onion (spring onion)
Onion read
Onion white

Orange
Orange juice
Papaya
Parmesan
Peaches
Peaches (canned)
Pepper Cayenne
Pepper white (ground)
Peppercorns
Peppers
Pheasant
Pineapple (from a can)
Plaice
Plum
Pomegranate
Pork stomach
Pumpkin seed oil
Rabbit liver
Raisins
Rhubarb
Rice (fragrance)
Rice (whole grain)
Rice black
Rice flour
Rice malt
Rice red
Rice sweet

Rice variety any
Rose hip tea
Sago (cereals)
Salt
Seacrab
Shrimp
Sorrel
Sour milk cheese 20%
Soy sauce
Soybean oil
Spinach
Spiny lobsters
Star anise
Sugar brown
Sugar white
Tomato
Tuna
Turkey breast meat
Turmeric (yellow root)
Walnuts
Watermelon
Wheat beer
Wheat bran
Wild boar meat
Yarrow tea
Yogurt (natural, 1.5% fat)
Yogurt (natural, 3.5% fat)

10.4 Do not use contra-acting foods

Basil
Basil (fresh)
Black tea
Boxhorn clover seeds
Cereal coffee
Chicken liver
Chili (pod or ground)
Cinnamon ground
Cinnamon sticks
Cocoa
Coffee
Corn silk tea
Curry
Feta cheese
Garlic
Ginger powder
Goat
Goat and sheep's milk
Goat cheese
Green tea
Herring
Hyssop
Juniper berry
Lamb bones

Lamb meat
Lamb shoulder
Lemon
Lemon juice
Lovage
Mold cheese
Mutton
Mutton
Nutmeg
Oregano dried
Parsley
Peppers (rose peppers)
Pimento
Poppy
Pork liver
Radish
Red wine
Rosemary
Sake
Thyme
Vinegar (Apple vinegar)
White wine
Yogi tea

11 Complementary

11.1 Cannabis seeds

Cannabis sat. Sem.
Preparation: Different effects
Nourishes juices, moisturizes bowels. Moisturizes intestines, relieves spleen, tones Yin, moisturizes.
Note: The absorption of other medicines taken at the same time may be slowed or hindered. Overdose may cause nausea, vomiting or diarrhea.

11.2 Hibiscus

Althaea
Preparation: Healing tea (infusion)
Nourishes Kidney-Yin and Lung-Yin, Derives Void-Heat, Nourishes Stomach-Yin, Cooling, Moisturizing.
Active ingredients: cane sugar, pectin, many minerals

11.3 Linseed

Linum, sem.
Preparation: Cooking addition
Moisturizes and relaxes intestines, clears heat, tones qi. Clarifies emptiness-heat by yin deficiency. Clears heat in the stomach and intestines. Moisturizes intestine.
Dosage: Simmer 2-3 teaspoon whole flax seeds with ½ liter of water for 10 minutes and allow to swell for a further 20 minutes and allow to cool. Take it in hot drinks, soups, warm dishes.
Note: The digestive effect is greatly enhanced if the seeds are well chewed. For children from 6-12 years halve the dose.

11.4 Sage

Salvia
Preparation: Healing tea (infusion)
Expels Mucus, Dries, Guides Down, Activates Wei Qi, Strengthens Qi. Essential oils containing many bitter substances and tannins should not be overdosed in order not to pollute the stomach.
Note: Do not use on: Pregnancy

12 Basics of Nutrition

The basic principles of nutrition described herein are general recommendations. They are not aimed at a specific form of therapy. Recommendations concerning a therapy have priority.

12.1 Nutrition

Regular meals in a relaxed atmosphere. A warm breakfast is considered a good start into the day.
The main meals ought to be taken for lunch – supper in the early evening. Pay attention to feeling hungry or sated: don't eat too much nor remain hungry is the rule
Prepare the meals freshly from natural, regional products. Frozen, heat-conserved, industrially prepared or foodstuffs cooked in the microwave oven are rejected.
Choice of foodstuffs according to the season: more cooling food in summer, more warming food in winter.
Eat cooked food at least twice a day. Food and drinks ought to be lukewarm, never ice-cold or hot.
Raw vegetables, briefly cooked vegetables, freshly squeezed juices and mineral water are not recommended. Milk and dairy products are only included in the diet if they don't cause problems.
Don't use therapeutic recipes over a longer period without consulting your doctor or therapist.

Varied food
Enjoy the diversity of foodstuffs. Characteristics of a balanced nutrition are variety, suitable combination and a balanced quantity of rich and low energy foodstuffs (on one hand avoiding undersupply with essential nutrients and on the other hand to take to many undesirable substances).

A lot of Cereal Products - and Potatoes
Bread, pasta, rice, cereal flakes (best wholemeal) as well as potatoes contain almost no fat, but many vitamins, mineral nutrients, trace elements, roughage and secondary plant substances. These foodstuffs ought to be taken with low-fat side dishes.

Vegetables and Fruit – „Take Five" every day …
5 portions of vegetables and fruit a day, as fresh as possible, briefly cooked, or maybe one portion as a juice – ideal as a side dish to every meal as well as snack between meals: Thus a lot of vitamins, mineral nutrients as well as roughage and secondary plant substances

Daily milk and dairy products

Milk and Dairy Products every Day, once or twice per Week Fish; meat, sausages as well as eggs moderately. These foodstuffs contain valuable nutrients like calcium in the milk, iodine selenium and omega-3 fat acids in saltwater fish. Meat is favorable due to its high content of disposable iron and the vitamins B1, B6 and B12. Quantities of 300 – 600 g meat and sausage per week are sufficient. Prefer low-fat products, especially in meat- and dairy products.

Low-fat and fatty Foodstuffs

Fat supplies us with essential fat acids and fatty foodstuffs contain also fat-soluble vitamins. Fat is high in energy; therefore much fat in the food may cause overweight, possibly also cancer. Too many saturated fat acids may further a tendency for cardio-vascular diseases in the long term. Prefer vegetable oils and fats (e.g. rapeseed-, olive-, soya-oils and solid fats produced therefrom). Beware of invisible fat in meat- and dairy products, pastry and sweets as well as in fast-food and convenience foods. 70 – 90 g fat per day is sufficient.

Moderately Sugar and Salt

Take sugar and foods/drinks containing various kinds of sugar (e.g. glucose syrup) only occasionally. Use herbs and spices as well as a little salt creatively. Prefer salt containing iodine.

Plenty of Liquids

Water is absolutely essential. Drink 1-2 l liquids every day. Prefer water (with or without gas) and other low-calorie drinks. Alcoholic drinks should not be taken.

Tasty Dishes, carefully cooked

Cook the meals with as low temperatures and as short as possible, using little water and fat – this preserves the original taste, keeps the nutrients intact and prevents the production of harmful compounds.

Take time and enjoy the food

Take your Time and enjoy your Food
Eating consciously helps to eat right. The eye enjoys food, too. It's fun, invites to enjoy varied dishes and stimulates the feeling of satiety.

Watch your Weight and stay in Motion

A balanced diet and a lot of exercise and sport (30 – 60 min/day) are a healthy combination. The right weight furthers well-being and health. Thermals, directional effectiveness, digestive power

There are various criteria for judging the effectiveness of herbs and foodstuffs.

The use of certain herbs and ingredients is based on observations of the effects on the body which these foodstuffs, herbs and spices show after having eaten them. The medical science has developed following system: Every ingredient or herb has a directional effectiveness. Furthermore, there are herbs which have a special effect on certain organs.

The basic condition for a healthy metabolism is to obtain sufficient energy from food and that the digestive process doesn't use too much energy.

An easily digestible meal makes content and sated, doesn't cause flatulence and fatigue after the meal. The perfect spices increase the healthiness of our meals. Very often, just small doses of herbs and spices will suffice. They are not used to make us sated, but to help our digestive organs to digest the food.

12.2 Recipes

The recipes list the ingredients to be used and the cooking instructions show how the dish is prepared. The list of ingredients shows the concerned quantities as well as the relevance for the therapy. If you find „less than mentioned", try to comply or find an alternative from the „list of recommended foodstuffs". Mostly it shall result just in a small change of taste when you simply avoid this ingredient.

Mild cooking methods: boiling, stewing, poaching, steaming
Strong cooking methods: barbecuing, roasting, frying, smoking
Balanced cooking methods: deep-frying, baking brick
Deep-freezing and warming in the microwave oven should be avoided (denaturalization).

12.3 Foodstuffs

Foodstuffs have an effect on body and soul like medicinal herbs, only a very much milder one. Dietary advice is mainly based on regional foodstuffs. The knowledge about the effects of each foodstuff and the knowledge, when which foodstuff shall be used, is based on the orthodox school of medicine. Use ecologic-organic products, if possible. As everything should be cooked for a long time due to a better digestability and very rarely eaten raw, the food agrees with everyone.

The classification of the foodstuffs according to their effect on the body is the basis in order to achieve a harmonious status of health.

Dietary advisors do not recommend certain foodstuffs for everyone. The individual diet is tailor-made for the individual constitution.

Buy only fresh and ripe fruit and vegetables. You ought to leave unripe fruit and vegetables and such with brown spots and wilted leaves behind in the market. In this case take deep-frozen goods (never ready-to-serve dishes!). Fruit and vegetables are deep-frozen immediately after harvesting and often contain more vitamins and minerals than the goods from the vegetable shelf. Whereas conserved or tinned goods contain very much less biological substances. Also, salt, sugar and others are mostly added to the latter. Never leave the foodstuffs in the water after washing them to avoid that many vital substances get drowned. Clean salads, fruit and vegetables immediately before serving.

Please make sure of the hygienic processing of foodstuffs. Clean your salads, fruit and vegetables carefully. When cooking with meat, prepare all ingredients first and then process the meat products. Clean the worktop and tools very carefully. Wooden surfaces ought to be treated with a mild disinfectant regularly in order to reduce germination.

Store fruit and vegetables separately, if possible. Harvested fruit and vegetables are still alive and emit e.g. ethylene gas, which makes other products ripen and age faster. Keep meat and fish in the closed packaging or store them in the fridge in closed containers.

12.4 Herbs

There are some basic rules for storing medicinal herbs. On principle, herbs must be protected from direct sunlight, humidity and heat.

Containers for the storage of herbs may be glasses, ceramic jars and even plastic containers. However, plastic is a rather unsuitable material and should only be a short-term solution. In case of glass containers, use a dark material.

Medicinal herbs cannot be kept for any long period. The shelf life of herbs is limited. However, it can be prolonged with suitable storage. The place should be dark, rather cool and absolutely dry. A wooden medicine cabinet, placed not directly next to a source of heat, would be ideal. Never buy large quantities of herbs so as not to have to throw them away. Label the container with the name of the herb and the date of harvesting or processing.

13 Other dietic-books

The following syndromes of dietetics, TCM or for a therapy supplement for cancer are available.

Dietetics

E001. Nutrition of the infant - baby food
E002. Nutrition during lactation
E003. Nutrition in old age
E004. Nutrition of children and adolescents
E005. Nutrition of athletes
E006. Light weight
E007. Pregnancy
E008. Full food

Protein and electrolyte - kidneys
E009. (hemodialysis) dialysis treatment
E010. Acute renal failure
E011. Chronic renal insufficiency
E012. Nephrotic syndrome
E013. Kidney stones (nephrolithiasis)

Gastrointestinal tract - pancreas
E014. Acute pancreatitis (inflammation of the pancreas)
E015. Chronic pancreatitis (inflammation of the pancreas)

Gastrointestinal tract - small intestine and large intestine
E016. Acute obstipation (constipation)
E017. Chronic obstipation (constipation)
E018. Colon irritabile
E019. Diverticulitis
E020. Acquired lactose intolerance (lactose malabsorption)
E021. Fructose malabsorption
E022. Glutensensitive enteropathy (celiac disease)
E023. Colectomy
E024. Short Bowel Syndrome

Gastrointestinal tract - liver, gallbladder, bile ducts
E025. Acute and chronic hepatitis (inflammation of the liver)
E026. Cholelithiasis (bile stones)
E027. fatty liver
E028. cirrhosis

Gastrointestinal tract - Stomach and duodenal intestine
E029. Acute gastritis
E030. Chronic gastritis
E031. Stomach bleeding
E032. Ulcus ventriculi and duodenal ulcer
E033. Condition after gastric surgery

Gastrointestinal tract - oral cavity and esophagus
E034. Stomatitis
E035. Esophageal carcinoma (esophageal cancer)
E036. Refluosophagitis (heartburn)

Special diseases
E037. Phenylketonuria (PKU)
E038. Rheumatic joint diseases

Metabolism
E039. Obesity (overweight)
E040. Diabetes mellitus
E041. Eating disorders (underweight)

Fat metabolism
E042. Hypercholesterolaemia (increased cholesterol level)
E043. Hepatic Encephalopathy

Heart and circulation
E044. Arteriosclerosis (arterial calcification)
E045. Heart insufficiency
E046. Hypertension
E047. Hyperuricaemia and gout

Changed nutrient requirements
E048. In case of fever
E049. For malignant diseases
E050. After burns
E051. Radiation and chemotherapy

CANCER
E100. Pancreatic cancer
E101. Bladder cancer
E102. Blood cancer (leukemia)
E103. Breast cancer
E104. Colorectal cancer
E105. Gastric cancer
E106. Kidney cancer
E107. Esophageal cancer

TCM
E200. Bladder - moisture heat in the bladder
E201. Bladder - moisture and cold in the bladder
E202. Bladder - emptiness and cold in the bladder
E203. Large intestine - external cold affects the large intestine
E204. Large intestine - moisture heat in the large intestine
E205. Large intestine - heat blocks the intestine II acute
E206. Large intestine - dryness of the colon
E207. Large intestine - Yang deficiency (cold)
E208. Heart - Blood insufficiency
E209. Heart - Blood stagnation
E210. Heart - Fire
E211. Heart - Hot mucus clogs the heart pores

E212. Heart - Cold mucus clogs the heart pores
E213. Heart - Qi deficiency
E214. Heart - Yang deficiency
E215. Heart - Yin deficiency
E216. Liver - Ascending Liver Yang
E217. Liver - Blood deficiency
E218. Liver - Blood stagnation
E219. Liver - Moisture heat in liver and gall bladder
E220. Liver - Fire
E221. Liver - Gall bladder Qi-Empty
E222. Liver - Cold in the liver meridian
E223. Liver - Qi stagnation
E224. Liver - Wind
E225. Liver - Wind with ascending liver Yang
E226. Liver - Wind with blood anemic
E227. Liver - Wind with extreme heat
E228. Lung - Qi deficiency
E229. Lung - Mucus-moisture in the lungs
E230. Lung - Mucus-heat in the lungs
E231. Lung - Mucus-cold in the lungs
E232. Lung - Dryness of the lungs
E233. Lung - Wind-heat attacks the lungs
E234. Lung - Wind-cold affects the lungs
E235. Lung - Yin deficiency
E236. Stomach - Bloodstagnation
E237. Stomach - Fire
E238. Stomach - Cold with liquid
E239. Stomach - Nutrition stagnation
E240. Stomach - Qi deficiency
E241. Stomach - Rebellious Qi
E242. Stomach - Yin Emptiness
E243. Spleen - Heat and moisture attack the spleen
E244. Spleen - Coldness and moisture affects the spleen
E245. Spleen - Qi deficiency
E246. Spleen - Qi deficiency + Declining spleen Qi
E247. Spleen - Qi deficiency + spleen does not control the blood
E248. Spleen - Yang deficiency
E249. Kidney - Heart and kidney no longer communicate
E250. Kidney - Jing deficiency
E251. Kidney - Kidneys cannot receive the Qi
E252. Kidney - Qi is not stable
E253. Kidney - Yang deficiency
E254. Kidney - Yin deficiency

For further information visit di-book.com.

14 EBNS - Software for nutritional counseling

The main task of the database is to create personalized nutritional advice for each patient individually. The database was developed for Dietetics and Traditional Chinese Medicine.

The Database supports training and advices in the daily work routine.

The computer program provides lists of recipes, ingredients and herbs, which are given to the client. individually adjustable according to patient's request from whole food to vegetarians (lacto, ovo, ...). For every register there is an information sheet which can be given to the client. All texts can be individually designed.

The syndromes can be combined and result in an intersection of the recommended recipes and ingredients. The automated diagnosis for the TCM enables you to check your experience during the training as well as to confirm your diagnosis in the working day. You select several predefined symptoms and have the program automatically display the relevant syndromes.

How to work with the database:
Select the patient / client, select one or more of the syndromes you diagnosed and print the folder.

You can change all values, create new symptoms or syndromes, develop recipes, change or adapt ingredients and herbs to your findings. In simple client management, all relevant data about the person is stored. You get an overview of the past diagnoses and the development of the course of the disease.

As a consultant you save a lot of time when you print out the recipe, food and herbal lists for the recognized syndromes and give them to the clients. You can use this time for a personal conversation. With the database, dieticians and nutritionists can view the nutrients and trace elements for each recipe and develop recipes for syndromes even with suggested ingredients.

All recipe and grocery lists can also be ordered from me as a combination of several diseases. I wish all readers good luck, health and happiness in life.
More information can be found at www.ebns.at.
Volunteer: www.krebsinfo.at
Josef Miligui